HARLAND LEARNS TO DRAW

Weird&Wacky

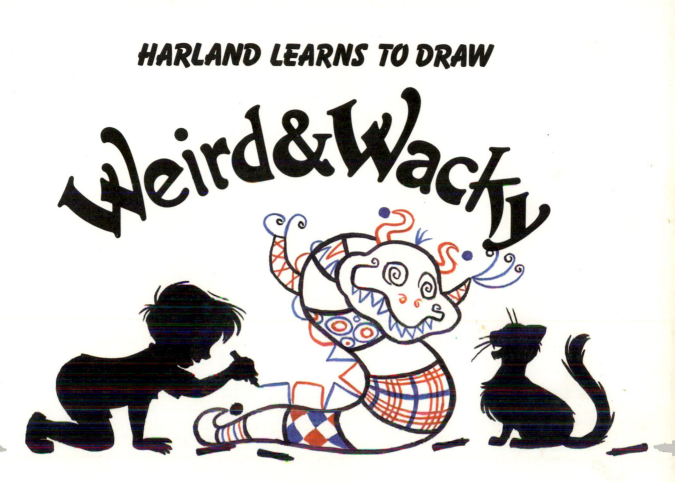

By: Andy Bartlett
Editor: Margaret Wood

Cyril Hayes Press Inc.
3312 Mainway, Burlington, Ontario L7M 1A7
One Colomba Drive, Niagara Falls, New York 14305

Hi! I'm Harland and this is my cat, Corky.
As you can see, Corky and I like to doodle.

Today we're drawing weird and wacky creatures.

Get out your coloring pencils and do your own doodle.
How many wacky things can you doodle in one doodle?

The easiest way to draw is to start with simple shapes.

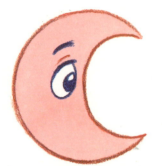

Let's start with a shape like this. Give it an eye. Add a nose and a mouth.

Give it some hair...
and a weird and wacky tie.

Presto!
Now you give it a try.

When there is something I want to draw, I sketch its basic shapes first. Use your pencil very lightly so you can erase your mistakes.

When it looks like you've got it right, fill in the details with your coloring pencils.

When I see a creature, I first look at its basic shape, its head, its body, its feet. I draw shapes in pencil so I have an outline.

Then, step by step, I fill in the rest. Make sure you erase your rough pencil lines. When you draw this way, even difficult things become easy.

If I want to draw action such as running, I start with a stick character.

No, Corky, a runner leans forward, so make the stick lean forward.

This is called using a line of action.
See, my character looks more like
he's running.

Now you add shapes to the line of action. Be
sure to curve them along your action line.

Add details like these
curved lines and blobs of sweat to
show that your character is on the move.

If you draw your figure just above ground level,
it will look like he's moving very fast!

A character's feelings run through its whole body.
These feelings are shown in the line of action.

Pride   Anger   Sadness

the nose in the air   the forward stance   the drooping head

Now draw the line of action for a person who is jumping for joy!

To help me get the line of action, I act out the pose in front of a mirror.

Another good idea is to look for a similar pose in a book or a magazine.

When you are ready to color your drawings, use weird and wacky colors.

What's that, Corky? You don't know what weird and wacky colors look like?

Well, they look something like this!

You can change the way the character looks by changing its proportions.

For example, when I want to draw a cute character, I draw the eyes big and low on the head.

I make the head big and the body small.

See, Corky, look how cute we are.

When I want to make a funny creature, I give it weird and wacky proportions. Why don't you draw your mom in a funny way. Then hang it up for everyone to see!

To draw a scary character, make the body big and the head small. Draw the eyes near the top of the head.

You have to be very careful when drawing scary characters though, because you can scare yourself.

Quick, let's get off this page in a hurry, Corky!

Notice Harland's line of action, the curved lines and sweat.

Sometimes, when I can't think of any
creatures to draw, I just make things up.

You can put the head of one animal on the body of another, like my caterpuppy, or join animals with things around the house, like my eleteapot. See how by adding a face to that chair it comes alive? What can you bring to life?

When drawing weird and wacky, always use plenty of imagination. Why not create your own weird and wacky world!

Look, Corky, Dad's home. That gives me an idea. Let's draw what a space parent driving to work would look like.

These creatures are too small to see,
Corky, but they live on the tips of your
whiskers. If I were you, I'd go have a bath!

These are the filthiest beasts I can draw. I call them scrungies. They live only in chimneys and at the bottom of mud puddles. Can you draw anything yuckier?

Now I'll draw us as creatures, Corky. You're a Catfish and I'm a Harlasaurus.

I don't think Corky likes being this weird and wacky.

So you're drawing me weird and wacky now, are you, Corky? Well, two can play at that game!

Now that you're an expert like us, you can try different ways to draw.

How many ways can you think of to draw one character?

After a long day of drawing, I hang up my favorite

weird and wacky pictures so that everyone can see them.

They also keep the real weird and wackies away at night.